CONTENTS

INTRODUCTION

Every day I thank God for all the people who are important in my life; the wonderful friends who reflect myself back at me with all my imperfections and make me smile at myself, at my insecurities, as well as rejoice with me in my moments of happiness and triumph. My life has been touched by so many extraordinary people, some who I have only met briefly, some whom I've known forever and others who have resurfaced in my life when I have needed them most. Our shared experiences have made me laugh and cry and I will be forever thankful to them for being a family to me when family weren't around or when family were too close to give me objectivity.

This book is about life, about those we love and losing loved ones. It's about the human condition and the extraordinary moments in our lives. This is largely my story, my journey to help me make sense of me but I feel it mirrors the lives of so many others. It takes a heartfelt look at the many stages of our lives, it reflects upon our insecurities, embraces our finest moments and our graceful (or even disgraceful) surrender of our youthful years. Life experiences mould and shape us...hardships and hurdles strengthen us and we come to terms with adversity, divorce, death ...we are designed like that. We all have an inner strength, a strength which sustains us from the inside when all else falls away.

This book looks at the humorous things which happen in our day to day existence. Sometimes it looks at how bitterness and blame can creep into our psyche and impact on our happiness and wellbeing and sometimes it's a reflection on the loss of those we hold dear. It's a timely reminder to cherish those closest to you and not hold them at arm's length without frequent reminders of what they mean to you.

I have been very privileged to travel and work in some fascinating places and learn about the traditions and cultures of some amazing people. People who despite having very little in the material sense, enjoy life to the full.

I would like to thank all my tremendous friends, colleagues, fellow writers from Burnley and District writers group, in particular Andrew Hamling, who has led me patiently through the process of self publishing! I would like to thank family who have given me inspiration for my poems and believed in my ability to follow this dream to completion. I have many treasured memories and experiences. I hope this book helps you to make sense of yours.

I dedicate this book to my mum and dad for their unwavering love of life and unfailing support, to my children Ben and Mark, to my loving, supportive partner Ray, to my family who have always been there to help me, my best friend Barbara who always tells me the bad side of things as well as the good, to my grandchildren who have all their life experiences to come and finally to Keith who opened his home to me whilst I gathered my initial thoughts for this book. Thank you all.

Welcome to this World

BIRTH

In awe I held you,
My wonderful new life.
You were a stranger to me,
Yet I knew you.
Your heart beat, not in a rhythm close to mine
And yet familiar.
Your eyes searching,
Questioning your place in my life.
Tiny fingers curled around mine.
And in that moment I so knew
That cutting cord would not cut through.

YOUR WORLD
(PRAYER FOR MY GRANDDAUGHTER)

May your world be filled with raindrops
to wash away your tears.
May life bring health and happiness
throughout your growing years.
May your angels bring serenity,
a heart that's filled with peace.
And may it be within a world
where war and conflicts cease.

May your intuition guide you
to achieve your hopes and dreams..
so nothing is beyond your reach..
however far it seems!
With bigger hands to catch you
every time you fall
strive for the impossible
you can have it all!

In a world with much uncertainty
there's one thing that holds true..
no one can ever love you quite as much as we all do.

DANCING WITH LIFE

Dear Carys,
I want to be young like you,
Race the wind.
Kick brazenly the gilded leaves.
Eat chocolate cake for breakfast.
Surround myself with beauty.

I want your thirst for knowledge
Perpetually ask questions..
Why this? Why that?
Feel the energy of giant waves
overpower me.

I want to believe in life like you do
Sink my teeth into it, sucking its sweetness.
Absorb the morning sunshine.
Live life on a tightrope,
exercise rebellion at every turn.

I want to explore the world like you will,
Sample parmesan crusted croissants
in some quaint Parisian street cafe.
Have champagne mornings and tender goodnights.
Dance with the stars under a Keralan night sky.

Instead I sit, an ancient oak
Old age wrapped around my limbs.
Little things loom larger now.
Fragmented thoughts congeal.
Time lies heavy.

All the glitter I reserve for company gone.
The mask of laughter stripped away.
Please talk to me.
I don't want to depart in a veil of silence.
My body sanitised, manoeuvred into a semblance of sleep.

WHILST YOU SLEEP

Whilst you sleep I watch.
Damp curls fringe your youthful face,
tussled, untamed.
Your small frame curled, embryonic,
free from worldly cares,
no sense of me or my conjecture.
A flighty breeze lifts filigree curtains.
You jolt,
flaying as a startled cat,
then reposition into an ever tighter ball.
Soon you will cast off my proffered hand,
too old for me to chide,
too knowing for my advice.
I cannot guard you from life's imperfect ways,
shield you from disappointment and rebuke.
I can only stand at a distance.

Love is Fragile

LIFE ISN'T BEAUTIFUL EVERY DAY

Life mellows and shapes who we are......challenges our very being and seeks out our soul. We are hardy and have learnt to take the knocks, the disappointments, the hurts. We have developed strength of spirit to shield ourselves against misfortune and pain and to bear those pains in relative solitude. We are all unique with the potential to make our mark in the world. Who are you in the presence of others? What makes you come alive? I have come to believe that personal growth demands a temporary surrender of security and we sometimes pay dearly to learn about ourselves what others can see at a glance! We wage significant battles within ourselves when it would be so much easier to go with life's rhythm, stand in the sunshine, free from self doubts and inner conflicts, believing in our ability to flourish and succeed as life intended.

FIRST LOVE

We were so young when first we met,
I know our love I'll not forget.
You awoke my passion, stole my heart,
I thought that we would never part.
You were my morning, noon and night,
The one I loved to hold me tight.
You shared my laughter and my tears,
Through those short but precious years.
Some inner feelings we never shared,
But I knew you always cared.
But love is impatient, and young love can't wait,
And destiny stepped in and decided our fate.
And though our lives grew far apart,
I remember the good times with all my heart.

NO TEARS

Robbed of ambition, love and years,
They made me hide my youthful tears.
Her final moments not mine to see,
They took those too away from me.
Desolation and anger buried inside,
A cut so deep, a cut so wide.

Robbed of exuberance, youth and grace,
That voluminous smile upon her face.
A career carved out, not mine to see
They took her future away from me.
Bitterness and sorrow inside my head,
My best friend gone, my best friend dead.

MARRIAGE
The Dream

When you are young and single
you live a carefree life.
You have romantic notions
of being the perfect wife.
You have no inclination
that marriage isn't bliss.
You imagine that all conflicts
can be resolved with a loving kiss!
You envisage your perfect children
playing and having fun..
whilst you cook your welcoming dinner
for hubby..your number one!
He never forgets your birthday.
He showers you with kisses.
If he's away on business
you know it's you he misses.
Oh what a dream you treasure
of blissful married life...
now let's face reality, my girl..
there is no perfect wife!

The Reality

You slave away to cook him grub
Whilst he wallows lazily in the tub..
Calling you to bring a beer..
'I'm thirsty love – can you not hear?'
Whilst watching footy on the telly
he needs more snacks to fill his belly.
His tum gets bigger by the day..
those tanned, toned abs have gone away

He queries money that you've spent..
'We need that money to pay the rent.'
And, 'Why do you need another dress?
It's only me you need to impress!'
Those endearing compliments you used to hear
no longer whispered in your ear.
If you are ill and take a sickie..
That's the day he'll beg for a quickie!
Housework isn't on his agenda
he'll feign work, then go on a bender..
Coming back all tender and sweet
forcing you to admit defeat.
Those indulgent moments to relax and unwind
are now incredibly hard to find.
Outings with the girls will stop
and supermarkets become your only shop.
You love your kids, they make you happy..
but constant tiredness makes you snappy.
Wherever is that girl of old?
This aging woman is a different mould.
Make some time to just be you.
They will learn to muddle through!

GROCERIES

Groceries are mounting.
They pile up day by day.
But we are dreadful hoarders,
Can't give them away!
Groceries are heavy,
Each bag weighs a tonne..
But we carry them all with us,
We can't offload just one.
The burdens of a lifetime,
The grudges we all bear
We all pile into grocery bags
and carry everywhere!

CANDY STRIPED BOX

His love
Came in a candy striped box,
Silk ribbon cascades,
Festooned with confetti hearts.
It felt light
With the air of anticipation,
Of snowdrops in the Springtime,
Candlelit dinners
And after dinner mints
Melting deliciously on our tongues.

Later
Love came in a carrier bag,
Worn at the edges,
Laden with groceries
Of a lifetime,
Carelessly discarded in a corner.
Neither one of us wanted to open it
Examine its contents
Mindful that to do so
It would have to go.

WHAT IS LOSS?

Loss is a cold December day in June
A starless sky without a moon
A fathomless sea which surges and toils
A venomous snake, curled and coiled
A grandfather clock which ticks no more
A , 'not at home,' sign hung on the door
Flames which burn from the inside out
That's what loss is all about.

GRAPPLING FORCES

A river stood between us
I stood on the opposing bank
Observing your meanderings.
A torrent of unspoken feelings
Laboured to break the surface
Whilst sun dappled water rippled mindlessly over rocks.
A strong undercurrent
Struggled to uproot the green algae.
We watched powerlessly
The river continue its downwards course
Towards a captive sea.

SULLIED PETALS

A heady scent of blossom filtered through the open window as Ali sat in front of her mirror willing herself to work up some enthusiasm for the day ahead, her wedding day. It was still relatively early in the day so an unusual quietness pervaded, allowing inadmissible thoughts to invade her consciousness, little darts poisoned with doubts and uncertainties for what lay ahead.

Alicia knew that it was too late to call off the proceedings, she wasn't that brave. In a few hours time she would be making her way down the aisle to become Mrs. Alicia Jane Alcott. Her dress taunted her from the side of the wardrobe, an ivory satin affair corseted tightly. She could feel it squeezing the life blood out of her before she even put it on.

Alicia wished desperately that these were pre-wedding misgivings but in her very being she knew it was not so. Suddenly upon saying yes her life had been commandeered. Wedding plans had morphed beyond all recognition. Alicia had once had a dream where she had drifted in and out of a series of rooms filled with people she knew. She had been privy to their conversations but all attempts to intercede had been futile. Alicia was a silent bystander, no one seeing or indeed sensing her presence. She felt like that now.

Alicia tried to take herself back to the beginning to where it had all started. She had been carefree, flirtatious in her dalliances with men no doubt. Men were drawn to her vivaciousness, it intoxicated them. She had had an energy she no longer possessed. Somehow she had exercised each morning before breakfast, stuck to her full agenda in her advertising job, managed drinks after work before settling down to complete assignments for her degree course to better her prospects. Marcus Alcott had been a client, smart and charming. It wasn't the 'done' thing to mix business with pleasure she knew that but Marcus wasn't a man to say no to and she found his intensity disarming.

Her life became a whirlwind of exotic dining, glamorous parties, vacationing in spectacular locations. Marcus loved to accompany her on shopping trips, helping her to select just the right outfit for an upcoming event. He chose her jewellery, found a more appropriate perfume. Alicia found herself wanting to please him, wanting to fit into this exclusive world of his. His family welcomed her and she became a regular at family dinners and gatherings. Merle, his mother, introduced Alicia to her own stylist and Alicia's hair was coffered into a style akin to her own.

The engagement was no surprise to anyone and everyone agreed they were a well matched, successful young couple. Alicia was momentarily caught up in the spell of it all but as the wedding arrangements were taken out of her hands Alicia began to realise that she had lost all sense of herself. Cracks had appeared in her confidence and a sense of getting caught up in the moment had gone. The essence of Alicia had leeched out to be replaced by a carbon copy, dull and lifeless in comparison.

Stirring from an adjoining room drew Alicia sharply back to the present. As she heard the door begin to open Alicia took one last look through the open window. This time she looked down. Blossom from the cherry tree lay carpeted around the tree itself. From afar it was a thing of beauty but up close you could see the colour beginning to fade, petals brown and curling at the edges. Some spark in Alicia died that day just like those sullied petals.

VITRIOL

Vitriol creeps insidiously within our veins,
A harsh reminder of life's injustices and pains.
A bitterness which permeates,
A bitterness with power,
A bitterness so cutting....
It's waiting to devour.
Thoughts fester with destructive force,
A rocky road, a downhill course.
Shadows creep in silently
And wrestle with your mind...
Resurrecting memories of dreams you left behind.
Darkness eats away at you
An emptiness inside,
The chasm ever deeper
The pain will not subside.
It threatens to consume you...
To eat you from the core,
A wicked, hungry predator knows what he's looking for.
The abyss ever deeper
Ablaze with weeping pain,
No thoughts of love can enter
For you to start again.

The Funny Side of Life

NOT MY BUM!

Snuggled together under the covers
Lie a married couple, bedtime lovers.
Duvet wrapped round them..
Feeling warm and rosy..but that all quickly changes
as they start getting cosy!
After a quickie...man rolls to the side..
advancing years have made him increasingly wide!
The duvet trails with him...
as he feathers his nest..
no lingering thoughts for his bare arsed guest!
Lying there in naked resplendour...
into arctic conditions he sends her!
Toes getting colder, frostbite encroaches...
bum get bluer as dawn approaches!
She can embrace some changes as she gets old...
but not a bum out in the cold!!

KNICKERS

Big knicks, thick knicks,
Get 'em off quick knicks.

Silky knicks, sweet knicks,
Right up your cheek knicks!
Lacy knicks, racy knicks,
Silly, sassy, crazy knicks.
Naughty knicks, shorty knicks,
Looking kinda haughty knicks!
Stringy knicks, flighty knicks
underneath your nighty knicks.

Thin knicks, sin knicks...
Chuck 'um in the bin knicks.
Cool knicks to school knicks,
Get the guys to drool knicks!
Cosy knicks, dozy knicks,
Bum getting rosy knicks.
Flowery knicks, spotty knicks,
looking kinda grotty knicks.
Country knicks, town knicks..
like to pull 'em down knicks.

When you're young, knicks are fun
Skimpy ones just hug your bum!
When you're aging...hormones raging..
Bigger ones are more engaging!
Find the ones to suit the day..
Hide the cheeky ones away!

THE BIG KNICKER POEM

For that growing waistline
You must indulge
(if nothing else to hide the bulge!)
In one pair of big pink knickers
To hold in place
your little kicker.
They're made with elastic
That will expand
Far more than you've ever planned.

They are not sexy
They are not cute
They make you look like a beached whale to boot!

But do not despair
Despite the hottest weather
Pregnancy does not last forever.
So hold your head up with pride
For the wonderful life which grows inside.

As soon as you have given birth
Follow that diet plan for all its worth
Throw those knickers upon the fire
(certainly not destined to spark desire.)
Replace with a G-string...some call a thong
To keep you smiling all day long!

RAGING HORMONAL NIGHTMARE

We hate those monthly miseries
and all that they entail
but they come around like clockwork
those miseries never fail
to make your tummy bloated
your boobs so very tender
It's enough to make a teetotaller
Go on a real bender!
Panadol and Advil stay very close at hand.
If you want to talk to us
Be careful where you stand!
Pans can end up flying
If you touch on a raw nerve
You will get a punishment
You think you don't deserve!
So humour me my darling
Don't argue, groan or sigh.
Don't ask when food is ready
as you are passing by.
Sane men keep their distance
Nod, smile and acquiesce
Give compliments about your hair
or that beautiful new dress.
Be thankful that monthly miseries
Which make us sad and blue
Are reserved for us dear ladies
And not the likes of you!

FLAT PACK LOVING

My love life's on self service
As all the guys I know
Don't know how to be endearing
or to let their feelings show.
They can shout out at the tele,
Get in a real hot rage
But when it comes to loving
Well we're not on the same page!
They drown out all emotion
...it don't have a manly ring
And they have to be all macho
'Cos that's a,' real guy,' thing!
So I've put away my stockings
From the naughty knickers' shop
And swopped them for some pj's
With a drawstring that won't drop.
I'm working on self service, a little DIY
I plan on going solo
Till I find that loving guy.

TEACHER'S PLEA

I cannot come to school today
My splitting head won't go away
My neck is stiff, my voice is weak
I hardly whisper when I speak
My temperature is soaring high
It's 40 now- I'll say goodbye
I've rung in early to let you know
And now I simply have to go.

HEAD'S REPLY

It's your head here. Can you struggle in?
My staffing quota's very thin.
There's no one to take your class
I know I'm being very crass
But panadol will help you out
I'll tell the children not to shout
It doesn't matter you can't speak
I'll tell them that it's miming week.
Your temperature we'll try to cool
with ice packs or the swimming pool.
Before you pass out on the floor
Can I trouble you once more?
Have you a friend to help today
To make my headache go away?!

SLUGS - SLOPPY, LAZY, UNTIDY GITS!

Tidy your room
Please comb your hair.
What awful things are lurking in there?
Mould and disease
under your bed.
Are you taking heed of a word that I've said?
Personal hygiene
a cause for disgrace
Surely my son you are washing your face?
Conversation stilted..
Just grunts and moans
Though you have no problem with your mobile phones!
Music is blaring
It's shaking the flat.
Is there, my darling, any consideration in that?
Needing a taxi?
Why fork out cash?
Butter up mum and she'll help you dash..
Out to the nightclubs
'till the early wee hours.
Your energy here has remarkable powers! Missing the
curfew
No concept of time
Surely that's not my mum on the line?
I know the ringtone, I'm in deep shit
But I'm having fun so I will not quit.
I'll face the music when I arrive back
But she will forgive me before hitting the sack.

As you grow older have kids of your own
I shall remind you as you start to moan
Of this terrible breed, self-centred and lazy
With terrible habits which drive you crazy
I had so much trouble keeping you in line.
And now my son it's payback time!

ON REACHING 50

Your youthful days aren't over
Your pilot light's not out
You've still got lots of sparkle
and that's what life's about.
Attend those raves and discos
Music beating in your head
You have so much to live for
'cos you're a long time dead!
Throw away those slippers
Put your dancing shoes back on.
Start again your romance
with your special one.
Forget the old and creaky bones
Forget the greying matter
I'm over 50 now myself
and madder than a hatter.
We know you are a softy
Caring through and through
There is no life plan guidebook
The rest is up to you.
Make time for what's important
Your family and your friends
For humour, love and laughter
until your great life ends.

WAY TO A MAN'S HEART ATTACK

I don't dine on yogurt
diet coke or cottage cheese.
I don't hone in on garlic
every time I sneeze.
I put butter on my spuds
devour chips along with fish.
I don't count the calories
of every single dish.

I never eat rabbit salad
or healthy wholegrain rice.
It's not the diet for any man
It's just for wimps and mice.
I know the doctor nags me
tells me to take control
says there's way too much cholesterol
tucked in my tummy roll.

I listen so politely
to everything he says
commit it all to memory
and vow to mend my ways
I get up in the morning
vitamins in hand
start my daily exercise
stretching as I plan.

An exhausting hour later
hungry as a beast
I go in search of fodder
a huge enticing feast.
Awaiting is my muesli
a smoothie and a kiss
but let's get one thing clear
I've had enough of this.

So fry up lots of bacon
sausages and bread
because all that exercise
makes me dizzy in the head.
You can keep all your health food
drink wheatgrass by the glass
but to put it in a nutshell
I think I'd rather pass!

On My Travels

PULSE OF ZAMBIA

Zambia has a pulse, a primeval pulse, a pulse which courses through your veins. When we hear it we respond immediately as if that rhythm is being recalled. The African drums are heartbeats which reverberate deep in the parched earth, the earth knows the beat, we know the beat and the imperceptible seduction has begun.

There is a seduction in the rhythm of life here. The heat is mellow and lulling. Movement of its people is graceful as if nature itself dictates this. Women walk tall, a dazzling myriad of colour and pattern, carrying the heaviest of loads, effortlessly elegant. Away from the towns cars have not infiltrated this calm and in the evening the life of the insects bears this out. Chirping crickets sound out their own choral fanfare and croaking frogs stir their potential mates. Perfume from jasmine, jacaranda and frangipani complete the seduction with their headiness. Jacaranda carpets the avenues bold in its vibrant, lilac hue. In contrast frangipani, so delicate in colour, a blush of yellow sneaking out from the creamy white flower.

In the townships the Zambian people, their faces aglow in the firelight, bodies perspiring, begin the movement of the dance as onlookers become a part of the ritual, swaying in time to that African heartbeat. The dance begins with a beat, a slow steady beat reflected in the movement of feet. Quickly the music and song become empowered, energetic, as bodies leap skyward marking life experiences in their gyrations: sometimes encouraging abundant crops, sometimes in celebration of a wedding or marking a rite of passage, their dances the soul of Africa.

The mighty Victoria Falls has a thundering pulse, a smoke that thunders. Rising deep from the bowels of the earth, the waters sent gushing from the Zambezi River, rise again from the boiling pot. The noise is a deafening sound of the thunder gods. Below irreverent crocodiles lie smiling, biding their time, greedy eyes breaking the surface of the waters momentarily. The spray flays out at you as you meander through the rainforest. Trees tower above; timeless trees whose roots stand firm. They offer permanence in a country where life is taken readily by disease and poverty or the perils of nature.

The pulse of the wild is felt in the game parks of Zambia. It begins as you descend in a little plane from Lusaka into South Luangwa National Park. It starts as an imperceptible bubble of excitement, anticipation. You are scarcely aware that the awakening has begun.

Animals in their natural habitat live life in the raw. Survival governs their every movement. You hear the thundering of the drums echoed in the chase when the earth tremors or waters convulse in a confusion of hoofs and horns as animals flee their predators.

The evening gives way to a slower pulse when the heat of the day diminishes with the fading light. African night descends in raw drama, the colours of the earth briefly afire, pools of molten gold give way to smoky greys as night quickly descends and the earth takes its rest. Animals weary from the sun's intensive gaze wind their way to the water holes where they stand silhouetted in their momentary stillness.

My soul feels revived yet tranquil as I take my leave. Zambia has a soul and I know I will forever be connected to the spirit of this beautiful country in Africa.

ZAMBIAN CHILD

He stared wide eyed at me,
pupils darker than midnight.
Eyes with hungry questions
he knew I couldn't answer.
He had so many things to teach me.
I kept my distance.
He couldn't reach me.
I was too young to understand
the complexities of his foreign land.

In years to come
I'd understand his thwarted dreams.
So little he demanded of this greedy world.
Yet I looked away from him,
choosing to remember
only that engaging smile,
that gentleness of spirit.
His pride,
a unique gift to this world.

MOSI-OA-TUNYA

'Smoke that thunders.'
I hear your deafening roar
Feel your misty breathed spray
before your waterfall spa.
I wander through the rainforest,
Sweet scent of rain soaked vegetation,
Patches of dancing sunlight flicker
through an overhead canopy.
Light diffuses, colours brilliant and saturated,
Greenery – so many hues on an artist's canvas.
Shadows of souls shimmer.
I hear my own footsteps, monkeys screeching
at odds with one another.

And then you're here!
I stand transfixed on the edge of a precipice
above your raging waters.
You erupt, plummeting over a knife edge,
Your liquid torrent pounding the earth's floor.
I find myself holding my breath,
Despite your force an eerie quietness pervades.
An African fish eagle rises and swoops
down into your gorge, his very own flight of the angels.
I know deep down in your belly swirling waters bubble
'A boiling pot,' so aptly named.
White water rafters grapple with your force,
Man challenging the very power of nature.

Further downstream a lazy Zambezi River meanders its
course
Home to snorting hippos safeguarding their young
from eager young canoeists testing their skills.
Sun baked elephants cool cracked skin in less turbulent
waters.
Tall grasses sway in the late afternoon breeze,
revealing glimpses of perfectly camouflaged impala.
Jocular tourists end a perfect day drink in hand,
Lulled to a restful sleep on leisurely sunset cruises
soaking up Mother Africa in all her glory.

Tranquillity pervades downstream
But here where I stand there is no evidence of that
gentleness.
This mighty waterfall ancient as the land
Has dominion, a force uncontrolled by man.

JACARANDA

I stop where the Avenue begins
enthralled by your beauty.
Your lack of modesty delights me.
A child's garish canvas
stares back.
Bold blue-lilac petals
aspire to blanket out the sky.
The same cluster of trumpet blossoms
threaten to swallow up my feet.

As I venture on, flat winged seeds take flight
kamikaze fashion.
I bend to pick one,
woody and crisp to the touch,
its papery casing falls apart in my hands.
In contrast to the seed pods the feathery ferns so delicate.
I look up astonished to see
that slender trunk of yours holding
strong masculine arms.

On a milky-white moonlit night
no wonder Mitu chose you
to safeguard his priestess,
'Daughter of the Moon,'
on her mission.
A timeless mission instilling
wisdom, faith, triumph over evil.
You swoop in majestically,
your silver plumage glowing.

You sing your song
so long, so long.
Its melody resonates
in the humid night air.
It's time..
Perfumed with sarrapia,,
hair entwined with sweet jacaranda
Vicharachia takes her leave
away forever, glorious on your wing.

BAOBAB

At close of day you beckon me,
Medusa like, reaching out,
drawing me ever nearer to you.
I smile,
your powerful stance beguiling me.
I sit awhile, recalling stories of my elders
as thunder rolls across the sky,
rain feeding the parched earth.
Many feet have honoured you with their presence,
their weary footprints painfully etched on your gnarled
hands
and yet you stand steadfast against the failing light.
My friend,
Keeper of stories,
Holder of dreams,
One day you will vanish without a trace
Your ashes scattered on the winds.
Know that you will not be forgotten.
In the moonlight
I will sit where once you stood
And you will dry my tears yet again.

AFRICAN STORM

The air quivers in the heat of the day.
A sun-parched earth cries out for rain.
The leaden atmosphere
bears down on us all afternoon.
October – the suicide month they call it.

There is always stillness before the storm takes hold.
Women, babies clinging to their backs,
their bright chitenges a colourful contrast to the baked
landscape,
wind their way home before the storm takes hold.

Dark clouds gather momentum above us.
Breathless air begins to stir.
An electric tingle lifts my body hair
 as the growling thunder moves closer.

In an instant the storm hits,
rain taking centre stage, bouncing
off the dirt roads, until with full force
it gushes in torrents down the streets
filling the storm ditches until they overflow.
Lightning crackles above us, flashing to earth
with unbounded glory.
There is a sensual passion in this power of nature
which terrifies and yet in the same instant
holds you transfixed.

I move away from my lean-to and stand,
letting the wild, uncompromising rain take hold of me.
I can't recall how long I stand there, caught up

in the magnitude of that storm.
The noise drowns out all other sounds
as it ricochets off the tin roof.

A thunderous boom shatters the air, bringing me back.

As quickly as it came the storm vanishes.
A triumphant sun breaks through the clouds, eyeing
the soaked landscape with her dazzling glare, drying
out dirt paths and ditches.
Soon all evidence of the storm will vanish,
the sky, an uninterrupted blue
once again.

TSUNAMI

I visited those places.
Walked the same beaches,
oblivious of the tragedy to come.
So close to those hungry waves
I slept a dreamless, peaceful sleep.
No raging torrent then
To rip apart their houses
Hurl unsuspecting bodies high and savage.
Only gentle waves caressing the sand
a mother's touch of her child's hand.

I watched those people
Shattered by their loss
Rebuild their broken lives.
No demon of nature
No tormented waves
Could break their fighting spirit,
eradicate the honour of their souls.
In time a gentle wind would heal their wounds.
A quietness would return to those peaceful shores.

FORBIDDEN LOVE

I remember the day,
Remember that day.

Your sari, in trails of cornflower blue
That day, that day,
When I met you.
Your sari slipped,
Your shoulder bare,
Cascades of silken, ebony hair.

 Lips so still, a deep red hue
That day, that day,
When I met you.
Eyes which spoke
Though no words came,
I never got to know your name.

We stood a while, a brief goodbye
You watched me leave,
I heard you sigh.
You'd held your breath,
As I'd held mine,
Another time, another time.

ON A WATER TAXI

I saw her on a water taxi.
In stark contrast to the murky waters
of Alleppey,
A Bird of Paradise, swathed in apricot,
bangles slithering up her young arms.
Kohl eyes, a half smile, hair closely cropped,
accentuated her beauty.

We shared a smile

She had a quiet air of confidence
beyond her years,
a knowingness I could not fathom.
I found myself staring at the dot
centring her brow, 'Guru Jyoti.'
A mark of spiritual practice,
the inward eye.

We shared a smile

She observed me watching her,
serenity and grace personified.
Perhaps she inwardly reflected on my presence
here on the backwaters of Kerala.

We shared a smile

HER ABAYA

My mistake was to believe
she wore her abaya like a sentence,
Not cloaked in closed emotions
or repressed desires,
she walked tall, straight,
purposeful. A shayla framed her desert eyes, intense,
yet mischievous. She drifted past me,
a scent of smoky wood, floral bouquets
and sweet butter. She gestured

for me to sit, take tea.
Time did not cloud her days.
Tea was a ceremony ushered in, sweet and minty.
Baklava, paper thin, layered like lasagne
accompanied the tea. I wanted
to lick the last of the sticky honey syrup
from my fingers, but accepted the hot cloth
proffered by her maid.

These are my children.' Her voice and bearing
was one of pride.
'Um Sumaya, Um Rashid.'
She hugged each of them
as though she had not seen them
for some time, gesturing for them to go and play.

I listened to stories of her life, her travels,
the adversity of strangers.
She was not blind to disapproving gazes. People, she said,
did not understand the traditions of her life.
She made no apologies for her broken English
and I felt no desire to intercede, break the thread
of her animated stories.

When she had finished she arose
I moved towards her, my cheek
brushed against her alabaster skin.
I expected her to feel cool, but her warmth
surprised me.
Ma'a salama, 'Peace be with you.'

I felt her peace.
I took my leave.

A WOMAN'S WAR

The sound of gunfire battled against the incessant rainfall. No amount of rain could drive out the ugliness of this war. It sounded closer tonight as if it might be tearing into neighbouring buildings. The sky was lit in what was becoming an all too familiar scene. I was too exhausted now; night upon night had broken me. However had it come to this state of lawlessness? How had the oppression and unjust use of power turned the seemingly ordinary citizens of Libya into mindless killing machines? How would they justify these inhumane acts to themselves in future years? I fired out these loaded questions into the night. These horrors could never be undone.

' Haram, haram,'....against God, that is what it meant. Surely they realised this? And surely there was some other way to effect change.

I was a prisoner now, confined to the house, the walls closing in on me; too scared to venture out in case I was caught in the crossfire. But supplies were running short; the children grew tetchy deprived of contact with their friends and cousins as I kept them away from school.

I watched the people in the street, braver than myself, slinking back against the sides of buildings. Their faces greyed in fear and sleeplessness. They wore a wariness; sunken eyes, hollow of emotion stared back at me as if they sensed me watching them. They too were broken spirits; the living dead. I hadn't thought about death much, I was only thirty three, but now it crept in daily to taunt me. I questioned my blind faith as never before.

I missed our weekend trips to Jebel Akhdar. The roads snaked through the wild countryside, a dry arid landscape to some but to us it had a beauty all of its own. When we reached our destination the children would run ahead of us laughing, as we clambered up the rocky terrain out of breath to reach the caves where I would gaze down admiring the little yellow flowers awash in the sunlight, struggling for recognition amidst the prickly gorse bushes which outflanked them. The sky invariably a spotless blue, sometimes you would hear the cry of a hawk and look up to see it flying overhead, gliding in endless circles. On descent we would lay out our picnic rug and while away the afternoon tucking into fresh pitta bread sprinkled with sumac or za'atar, humus and olives, apricot juice and date cake, still warm from the oven. The late afternoon sun would bear down on us, warming us through, making us replete. Other times we would venture further afield to the historical site of Cyrene, overlooking the Mediterranean. Here we would hear the sound of our own footsteps as we meandered through those majestic pillars erected by our ancestors; the silence taking me back to another era. Here it was not the silence of repression it was the silence of peace and tranquillity. I liked to watch the light diminish, the horizon fade into nothingness and then we would take our leave taking with us a bit of that timeless beauty.

I longed for the commonplace activities, routine chores. I used to sing before morning prayers. Samaya, my daughter, would laugh as I forgot the words to familiar tunes but I didn't care. I longed for the normal; normal mornings taking the children to school, the incessant chatter which announced their arrival home, normal afternoons spent having tea with Samah, Shorouk and

Aya, after which we would walk Aya's twins in the park enjoying the warm sunshine of the late afternoon; the heady scent of blossom mingling seductively with oud wafting from our abayas.

Tears pricked behind my eyes now as these images crept into my consciousness. I felt my throat constrict. I mustn't wake the children, let them be privy to my inner turmoil ..my sense of hopelessness. I knew my children had already witnessed too much bloodshed in their short lifetimes, observed too many tears and yet they slept the sleep of the young secure in the knowledge we would protect them. Inshallah we would keep that promise. I bent to kiss my children, my lips lingering momentarily longer on Sumaya, my most sensitive child. Her heavy eyelids stirred sleepily, opening momentarily. Her raven hair framed her beautiful face..oh how I loved her. She smiled and in that instant I had hopes for tomorrow; hopes for many more tomorrows.

MEMORIES OF THE EMIRATES

Soft dry sands
Blow gently over the desert plains.
Warm winds whip up and swirl around me,
Enveloping me in a sense of timelessness.
Dhows glide majestically
Over the water
Creating a beautiful silhouette
Against the evening sky.

Wafts of exotic scent drift past me
Strong, pungent and powerful as their wearers.
Tall palms offer shade and resilience
Against the harsh, arid climate
Reminding me of the heritage
Of its nomadic people.

THE DOOR

The door never creaked. I didn't know how old it was, only that it was extremely heavy and outflanked me and my brothers and sisters; even Salim, who towered over me like the minarets merely came half way up .The door had always marked stages of my life. As a child I had never been able to open it and had relied on my parents to push it open on our return home. I observed it now, remembering the times Baba had scooped me up at its entrance announcing our arrival back from the family shop. The door hadn't changed over the years and showed no signs of wear and tear. It was finely carved in its arch with patterns of trailing leaves which cascaded in all directions, overlapping at various intersections. The vertical panels were adorned much in the same manner but interspersed with lotus blossoms and palm leaves, indicating that ours was a family home. Horizontally the door had brass spikes running along wooden panels which, to my child eyes, looked as threatening as the cactus growing ever taller in our courtyard. Some of the surrounding stone work, in contrast, was crumbling daily, showing signs of age and the paint on the building was flaked and crackled like my Teta's crumpled paper face, which I loved so dearly.

The street we lived on was narrow, never constructed to carry so many motor cars. Nowadays you can hear the incessant tooting of horns as irate drivers vie to push their vehicles into impossible spaces, forcing other less mobile road users to retreat hastily into neighbouring back alleys. In the day time the street is relatively quiet but at night it comes to life with street sellers calling out to passersby and cafes buzzing with infectious laughter, the air alive, modern Arabic popular music drowning out more traditional songs of lament. Combinations of sandalwood, musk, oud and jasmine fill the air as married couples and groups of young boys or girls walk along our street, a regular pastime of the young, not yet ruled by traditions and commitments. I had been one of those young people.

I remember being a timid child. I would hang onto the side of my mother's abaya frightened that if I lost hold I may be lifted high into the air by the shamal like the kites of my brothers, which danced gregariously, as if governed by unknown forces of nature. My mother said I had a vivid imagination. Unlike many of my cousins I went to school, my parents believing that an education was important for girls as well as boys. I loved the daily ritual of gathering up my belongings, which consisted of pencils and beautiful colouring pencils purchased by Teta, a snack of za'atar bread fresh from the oven with dates or other seasonal fruits, packing them into my small backpack and heading out with Jamal, my youngest brother, to our local school, where I would be immersed in gathering information about my country and the world beyond my front door. I listened attentively, rarely daring to ask questions, though I had so many and as the years passed I had so many more. I wanted to know why womens' voices were not acknowledged in any true sense in our culture and why women could not be part of the future decision making process in politics. My mother smiled at my questioning though never gave me an answer which satisfied any of my curiosities. This remained the same until the day Hamid entered my family home with his parents that hot summer in 2001.

Hamid was tall unlike his father. His shoulders were strong and muscular and when he smiled he unnerved me; it was as if he had direct access to my thought processing. I blush bright crimson, looking down embarrassed in case he'd been aware of me staring at him. My father introduced us and Hamid smiled again bowing his head respectfully. Hamid had finished school two years ago and now had a promising career in an up and coming environmental agency. He started telling my family all about his plans to get local schools involved in his venture to protect threatened wildlife species and to get younger students active in beach and park clean up campaigns. At first I was listening attentively to his every word but soon found myself regarding him physically in a way I had never done before with other sons of friends of my father. In time I was to know so much more about Hamid and his ambitions, there was so much more to know.

I met Hamid for a second time on my way back from school. Jamal was loitering with his friends so I went ahead swinging my arms in the afternoon sunshine. I remember his first words to me,

'Someone looks happy!'

Caught off guard I turned around to be met by those dark penetrating eyes.

'Oh yes. It's such a lovely afternoon. We rarely get these soft gentle winds at this time of year.'

Hamid caught up with me and we strolled back to my home conversing more easily about my days at school, future ambitions and general pleasantries which form a respectful expectation of Arabic conversation. At my door I hesitated, not wanting our time together to end. Hamid broke the silence as I reluctantly pushed open the heavy door left ajar in expectation of our return.

'Shall I see you tomorrow on your way home?'

'That would be nice,' I found myself replying.

My life took on a new pattern after that day. Jamal, sworn to secrecy, never gave me away. He had too many secrets of his own that he didn't want me to reveal either. My mother kept busy with Jamila, the new addition to the family never heard our protracted goodbyes as we rested ourselves against those sturdy wooden door panels. All the strong independent ideals I'd been harbouring about not falling into the love trap fell away in the company of this wonderful man who was fast becoming everything to me.

The summer I left school I felt different, confident and prepared to take on the challenges of the working world. Interviews were arranged by my father for an administrative position in the oil company where he worked. I sailed through the interview and dictation test and a date was set for me to start. Hamid sent me messages of good luck but our past regular meetings were much harder to orchestrate with my new working hours and the fact that my father now acted as chaperone, giving me a lift home each day. On hotter evenings I found myself sitting on my doorstep resting my back against that heavy, dependable door, gazing up at the night sky in the hopes that Hamid would just pass by to talk. I missed our talks so much. Hamid really listened to me as no one ever had.

The first time I saw Hamid after I started work was six months into my job. I left work early one day when my boss was due to take his annual leave. I had permission to meet up with Shorouk my old school friend in a cafe in the Mall. I was a little early so I began browsing the local shops looking for a gift for my cousin who was due to get married next month. I heard him before he saw me, that same familiar laugh which I loved so much. I turned around excitedly and our eyes met. He was not alone. Next to him stood a tall woman cloaked in less traditional abaya embellished with tiny diamantes. She smiled at me waiting to be introduced. Many thoughts went through my mind in that moment and I hoped beyond hope that Hamid would introduce his favourite cousin. What followed proved to be much worse. Hamid had the good grace to wait a minute for me to take control. Then he turned to the woman next to him, placing his big hands gently on her slender shoulders he introduced Hala, his future bride. Hala, with all the sweetness that her name implied, gently took my fingers in hers.

'I hope we will become good friends,' she said.

My mind rushed to find some suitable reply. I can't imagine what I said, so rude not to make a suitable response. I was not prepared for this. I must have made some excuse as I took my leave. I must have made polite conversation with Shorouk as I tried to muster up some of my usual spark.

I walked home that day despite the distance, despite the fact that it was not seemly to do so alone. I needed time, composure. I stood outside that imposing door breathing deeply before I knocked. Teta opened it, greeting me warmly. I put on my bravest smile as I greeted my family like long lost friends, as is our custom. So much I held back, they would never know.

So many years later as I sit in the chair where Teta used to sit I hear the door that never creaked. I smile. It's getting older too. Isra rushes in, holding out her backpack to me. She climbs up on my knee nestling into the rug which keeps my legs warm from the winter chill.

'Read to me,' she says.

I read and she asks me questions. I hope as she gets older I can answer them honestly, as my family rarely could.

I never made that difference to the wider world. I hope that I still had time to make it to mine.

CHRISTMAS MARKET

Ferocious the crowds that day
Misshapen bodies contort to make a run
on over-priced ware.
There are no bargains.
Everything for sale comes at a price,
Yet there is no shortage of customers,
so tantalising the array of goods.
It is not yet November
Yet Christmas hangs in the air
like a promise.

Necklaces of cream or black pearls
Woven together by silky ribbon snugly curl
into silk lined boxes,
Garish Winter hats resembling
creatures in the wild, transformed
by psychedelic colours and patterns
have strange eyes peeking out at you.
Lavender and sandalwood soaps and oils,
A blend of home and distant, mysterious lands
Combine to draw you intoxicatingly close.

Olives with pearls of garlic
Smelly cheeses with peculiar names,
Stinky bishop, Sgt Pepper, Shepherd's Hope and Fat
Bottomed Girls.
Hot smoked sausages drip fat
Into podgy fingers shaped like sausages themselves.
Cinnamon Christmas tree biscuits like ladies lace
adorn the market tables.
Gluhwein , sweet and spicy slides down gullets
warming and mellowing us
as we snuggle together in the tents.

Small children in colours as dazzling as peacock feathers
grip tightly to their parents hands.
I watch a small girl pick up a snow shaker
turn it over in her hands, feeling it's beauty lovingly.
To her it's something special and the price no longer
matters.
'Silent Night,' rings out into an air
raw and sharp
Stalls with little left to sell begin to pack up for the night.
The clamour quietens as the evening stars
pepper the sky.

BEING A BRIT

Loud mouthed football louts
Is not what England's all about,
Although that's the way that it may seem
When you turn on your TV screen.
It's people watching on the underground train
and regal black cabs in the driving rain
It's the hustle and bustle of life in the city
It's musicals, plays, so lively and witty.
Away from London the scenery changes,
Country cottages amidst beautiful mountain ranges.
It's seeped in history for you to explore,
Fine architecture, museums, cathedrals and more,
It's richness of culture a delight to behold
Regardless of age - you're never too old.
Venture off to Cornwall and Devon
Their cream teas will have you in seventh heaven.
Seaside resorts famous for fish and chips
Straight from the paper – get you licking your lips.
Visit those quaint little Inns, that we call a pub
With big log fires and tasty grub.
Our big red buses, milk at the door
The postman bringing letters galore
The amazing gardens with herbs and flowers
If I had enough time I'd go on for hours.
The changing of seasons is something I miss
Soft rain, blustery winds are my idea of bliss
The wonderful hues of crisp fallen leaves,
Descending on mass from the Autumn trees.
I see Britain through rose coloured glasses
But hope that vision never passes.

The Spiritual Side of
Life

THE LIFE INSIDE OF ME

I live my life inside my head,
I will not live as if I'm dead.
My light is kindled, shadows fade,
no longer will I be afraid
to be at peace, with me, myself..
our inner beauty is our wealth.

I mould my life, it is not cast,
I will not live for what is past.
My soul takes flight, my worries cease,
I seek inside for inner peace.
My strength of spirit sees me through.
My inner journey starts anew.

IN THE STILLNESS OF THE NIGHT

In the stillness of the night
You can count the stars as all your blessings.
You can search your soul for forgotten memories and
desires.
You can reach inside yourself
for inner guidance to this earthly existence.

In the stillness of the night
You can hear the whispering of the wind
Keeping company with the quiet moments
of your inner voice.
You can discover your inner child
and let her arms reach out to comfort you.

In the stillness of the night
You can heal the burdens of a heavy heart
created by the limitations of your thoughts.
You can refresh your soul
and learn to be at peace with yourself
in this world.

INSIDE MY SOUL

As the night begins to fade
I'd love to know for what you pray.
Your deepest dream, Your heart's desire
I'd love to know what sparks your fire.
We are but strangers passing time
Lives interwoven, intertwined.

As dusk bemoans the end of day
you seem so very far away.
Your hidden emotions, ghostly haunts
I'd love to know what grieves or taunts.
We are together, yet so apart
I need to know what warms your heart.

As seasons roll and rearrange
My life unfolds, and seeks out change
I search inside my soul to find
meaning from a life left behind.
Buried scenes all scurry past
like movies, never meant to last.

Pictures vivid in my head
So many things I left unsaid.
As I venture out once more
I know I'll not close any door.
An albatross with outstretched wings...
will soar in search of better things.

DEATH

He creeps in stealthily,
bereft of form.
We do not recognise him,
though we stand face to face.
He isn't greedy.
He steals time slowly,
only a miniscule part,
hardly discernible
except to a keen observer.

I HELD YOUR HAND

' My father moved through theys of we,
singing each new leaf out of each tree
(and every child was sure that spring
danced when they heard my father sing)..'

Poem by E.E Cummings

I held your hand, square, solid; perhaps not so remarkable in a man and yet you were remarkable. You squeezed back gently. The warmth of your hand remained a comfort; soon that too would pass. I knew you only had a little time left. I couldn't imagine a life without you. Your love, given so freely, would that die too? So many questions went through my mind in the days before you left us.

I remembered other times you'd held my hand, it had seemed so big and yet you had small hands for a man. You gripped me tight as I scrambled over rocks at the seaside, lifting me high as I giggled when boulders were too big for my small feet. You held my hand when we walked around the noisy fairground, I clung on tightly thinking that if I let go I may never find you again amongst the throng of people. You squeezed my hand that day you'd taken me for my first interview, giving me confidence and reassurance and when I walked down the aisle, a part of me didn't want to let go in case the new life didn't match up. I wish you were squeezing it now for a different reason.

The day outside was warm for May. Shrill cries from children out on the back lawn, little squabbles and incessant chatter made the final parting more bearable. The youngsters drifted in and out of the room, in many ways themselves and yet they knew something would change that day.

As I sat with you vivid images kept a steady stream of memories flooding back. You recorded all those childhood moments meticulously. You loved life, you loved to travel. You didn't need the photographs, the cine films you took, I knew you could bring to mind our first steps, the day we learnt to ride our bikes, my first ballet performance, our first sightings of those magnificent Victoria Falls, game drives in Luangwa Valley. I knew we had been the lucky ones; you loved to see places through others eyes more than your own. You told me it wasn't the same seeing amazing things if you had no one to share them with and I knew you were right.

On the day we buried you people on our street stood outside solemnly acknowledging our loss; race and creed no boundary to show respect for a man who'd touched their lives too. They bowed their heads as we moved past them on that interminable journey to say goodbye. How do you do that..say goodbye? We'd written words and poems, tried to capture the essence of our extraordinary dad, yet it was not quite enough. In the gathering after the service we remembered all those good times, the stories you told about your youth...even though we'd heard them a million times before and rolled our eyes they brought comfort now. I knew you'd want us to carry on as before, you were practical....death was as natural as life.

In the days after you'd gone I thought about the power of touch. We'd managed to lose some of that understanding of how healing it can be, no words necessary. I wanted to tell people to slow down, re-evaluate what was important. We detach ourselves from emotions. I wanted to tell people to embrace them. I knew your love would carry on , you had so much of it..how could it not? I realised also that you knew in those final days how much you had meant to us all as we held your hand.

YOUR FOOTPRINT

Your footprint will never leave us.

You gave us everything of yourself
And asked for nothing in return.
You scattered laughter like confetti
Allayed so many fears.
Your bigger heart made ours feel lighter in your presence
And when we walked a tightrope
You were there for us
To talk us through it
Or to catch us if we fell.
Without you life becomes more ordinary

Some men leave their footprints
Etched forever on others lives and one was you.

In our minds we see you plainly now
We hear your kindly voice
And know in certainty
The waiting world will flourish in your presence
As this scattered world will mourn your loss.

You were extraordinary.

DORIS

She sits in her chair
wrinkled with kindness.
Age resting on her shoulder
like a timid bird.
Hair whisper soft,
framing gentle parchment features.
Welcoming her offspring's offspring,
Whom she takes on wild adventures
of their imaginings,
whilst wrapping them tenderly
in her pillowy arms.
She laughs
and the years fall away
as effortlessly as the break of dawn.

Later they depart,
taking a little of Doris with them.
And she sits alone,
memories serenading her
till sleep takes over.

MY MUM

She was my mum
I knew her face
But not like this
not in this place.
I glanced upon her face awhile
Some comfort in her serene smile.
I bent to hold her fingertips
I brushed against her icy lips.
My heart inside was like a stone
And from my lips I heard a moan.
I should be brave, I should be strong,
I can't stay here very long.
I don't believe I said goodbye
I was so brave, I wouldn't cry.
Inside my body blood ran cold,
A young woman suddenly very old.
Where had her life, her laughter gone?
My mum I could depend upon
To hug me close when things went wrong.
I must be brave, I must be strong.
On the drive back to our house
I sat as quiet as a mouse
With vivid pictures in my head
It sank in that my mum was dead.
The flat inside was freezing cold
Not warm and comforting as old.
Mum's things were scattered all around
But not her voice and not her sound.
In my head her frequent calls
Echoed down those hollow walls.

Her scent it lingered on her clothes,
I held them up against my nose.
And as I slept in fitful dreams
I felt her loving embrace it seems
For as she held me in her arms
I felt a sudden sense of calm.
I knew then she would not depart
She'd be forever in my heart.

ON THIS EARTH

On this Earth we are as leaves
Stirred up in the morning breeze,
We twist and turn as we take flight
Are swept right up into the light,
Each tiny one of us unique
Reaching for the path we seek.

On this Earth we are as flowers
Touched by dew and morning showers
Soft - petalled beauties, God's own scent
In youth so proud, in age so bent
We blossom briefly, have our day
But we were never meant to stay.

Printed in Great Britain
by Amazon

24816931R00050